About This Book

Title: *Birds Around the World*

Step: 6

Word Count: 232

Skills in Focus: All vowel-r combinations

Tricky Words: build, baby, find, Earth, penguins, eyes, breath, feathers, mountains

Ideas For Using This Book

Before Reading:

- **Comprehension:** Look at the title and cover image together. Walk through the pictures in the book with readers and have them make predictions about what they might learn while reading.
- **Accuracy:** Practice saying the tricky words listed on page 1.
- **Phonics and Phonemic Awareness:** Prepare r-controlled vowel word cards with the words *burst*, *perch*, *twirl*, *over*, *under*, *world*, and *worm*. Have readers identify and underline the vowel-r combination for each word (e.g., the *ur* in *burst*). Read the words together several times. Ask readers, "What is the second sound in *burst*? In *perch*?" Point out that the sound (/r/) is the same, but it can be spelled differently. Other times words can be spelled *ar*, *er*, *ir*, *or*, or *ur*, but they still have the same the vowel sound, as in *form*. Tell readers that while they read, they will be looking for vowel-r words and listening to how they sound.

During Reading:

- Have readers point under each word as they read it.
- **Decoding:** If readers are stuck on a word, help them say each sound and blend the sounds together smoothly. Point out words with r-controlled vowels as they appear.
- **Comprehension:** Invite readers to talk about new things they are learning about birds around the world while reading. What are they learning that they didn't know before?

After Reading:

Discuss the book. Some ideas for questions:

- What different types of birds have you seen before?
- What do you still wonder about birds?

Birds Around the World

Text by Laura Stickney

Reading Consultant
Deborah MacPhee, PhD
Professor, School of Teaching and Learning
Illinois State University

PICTURE WINDOW BOOKS
a capstone imprint

Kinds of Birds

There are many birds around the world.

They live in different places on Earth.

Owls perch in dark forests under the stars.

Condors soar over mountains.

Robins perch on branches to build their nests.

They lay eggs that hatch into baby birds. Their babies eat worms.

North or South

Geese fly south for winter.
They form a letter V in the sky.

They go to warmer places far away.

Some birds
stay up north.

Chickadees adapt to cold weather.

Chickadees hide food that they can find later.

They warm their thick feathers in the sun.

Parrots

Parrots live in rainforests.
They have bright tail feathers.

They burst open hard nuts and seeds with their sharp, curved beaks.

Parrots help forests.

They drop seeds from the air into the dirt. New trees start to grow.

The Ostrich

The ostrich is the world's largest bird.

It can run fast and far. It can kick with force.

Ostriches survive in deserts. Their feathers blend in with the dirt.

They do not need to drink much. They get water from plants.

African Penguins

African penguins live on coasts. These birds hold their breath to swim.

They whirl and
twirl underwater.

Feathers keep penguins warm in freezing water.

African penguins have bare pink skin near their eyes.

When it gets hot, this bare skin keeps the birds cool.

Birds around the world are neat!

More Ideas:

Phonics Activity

Play Memory with Vowel-r Combinations:
Prepare two sets of cards (using two different colors) to play a game of Memory. On one set of cards, write vowel-r words from the story. For each word, prepare a separate card of a different color with the corresponding vowel-r combination. Place the cards face down on a surface. Have students take turns turning two cards over, one of each color. To make a match, the students must read the word on one card and have the matching letter combination on the other. Continue playing until all cards have been matched.

Suggested words:

- *ar*: dark, stars, sharp
- *er*: perch, feather, under, weather
- *ir*: bird, dirt, whirl, twirl
- *or*: forest, north, form
- *ur*: burst, curved, survive

Extended Learning Activity

Birdwatching:
Take students birdwatching outside. Ask them to observe the different birds they see and the different bird calls they hear. Then have them write a few sentences about their observations on a piece of paper. Challenge readers to use words with vowel-r combinations in their sentences.

Published by Picture Window Books, an imprint of Capstone
1710 Roe Crest Drive, North Mankato, Minnesota 56003
capstonepub.com

Library of Congress Cataloging-in-Publication Data is available on the Library of Congress website.

ISBN: 9798875227240 (hardback)
ISBN: 9798875231278 (paperback)
ISBN: 9798875231254 (eBook PDF)

Image Credits: iStock: Artush, 20–21, Naomichi Okawa, 8, slowmotiongli, 23, THEPALMER, cover, USO, 24; Shutterstock: D.serra1, 30, Dejan Lazarevic, 16, Evannovostro, 10–11, FrentaN, 4–5, Izzet Safer, 7, Jessica 1987, 6, Jim Nelson, 14–15, John Quintero, 2–3, JOMI - Joe Alvoeiro, 12–13, JT8, 32, Kcuxen, 25, Martin Mecnarowski, 18, Mike Truchon, 9, Neil Bradfield, 26–27, R J Endall Photographer, 17, Sergei25, 22, Sergey Uryadnikov, 1, 28–29, Unady, 19

Printed and bound in China. 6274